GRACE AND GUTS TO LIVE FOR GOD

A BIBLE STUDY ON
HEBREWS, I & II PETER

GRACE &
GUTS
TO LIVE FOR GOD

LES MORGAN
ILLUSTRATED BY RON WHEELER

HORIZON BOOKS
Camp Hill, Pennsylvania

Horizon Books
3825 Hartzdale Drive, Camp Hill, PA 17011

ISBN: 0-88965-121-3
LOC Catalog Card Number: 95-77842
© 1995 by Les Morgan
All rights reserved
Printed in the United States of America

95 96 97 98 99   5 4 3 2 1

Cover and inside illustrations by Ron Wheeler

CONTENTS

FOREWORD

Over the past 15 years, I have been blessed with the opportunity to be involved in the Bible quizzing program where young people memorize a specific book or books of the Bible for each quizzing year. As part of the program, our young people are also encouraged to use a Bible study book to help them with the in-depth study of the material and learn how it can apply to their lives. I am thrilled that Christian Publications is publishing a book on Hebrews and First and Second Peter, which are part of the Bible quizzing cycle. It will be a great study aid for us as part of the Bible quizzing program.

The title of the books says it all. It does take "grace and guts" for today's young people to live for God and stand up for their faith. The pressures that young people are facing in today's world are not much different from what Christians faced in the first century. They too were under pressure to abandon Christianity and needed encouragement to live holy lives in a world filled with impurity.

This book does an excellent job of explaining concepts from the Bible text by providing applicable examples on current issues and asking the reader to respond to challenging questions. Even if you are not involved in a Bible quizzing program, this is an excellent book to use for a group or personal Bible study program. It will give you a biblical perspective for your everyday life and show you the necessity of studying, learning and applying scriptural principles to become a more active, knowledgeable disciple of Jesus Christ.

Tony Kong
Director of Bible Quizzing
Pacific Northwest District
The Christian and Missionary Alliance

PREFACE

It takes guts to live today!

Gang violence is at an all-time high. Reports of drive-by shootings are in the news nearly every day. Car hijackings are not uncommon. Every day 150,000 students carry guns to school. Marriages and homes are splitting apart at a pace never known before. The music industry is "going to the bank" on rap songs that promote immorality, selfishness and even cop-killing! Wimps don't have a chance.

To survive in a world like this takes grace and guts! Thankfully, God has plenty of both. He has always been there to meet people in their darkest hours. In this study of Hebrews and First and Second Peter, you will see that firsthand. Jesus promised He would never leave or forsake us (Matthew 28:20; Hebrews 13:5). He makes good on His promise!

The great news is this—no matter what difficulty has invaded your world, the Lord will bring you through. He won't stand to the side with His arms folded across His chest watching to see if you can fight your way through the pain. Not our God. He will give you all the grace and guts you need to face whatever comes. He will see you through! Let's study and grow in that.

INTRODUCTION

Imagine growing up being hated because of what you believed about God. Think what it would be like to be threatened constantly and despised because of the faith your family practiced. Everywhere you went, people would be taking cheap shots at you. Leaving your family roots would be the most destabilizing thing you could do, for to do so would not only cause further conflict with those who already hated you, but would also bring an avalanche of anger on you from your family as well!

In essence, Hebrews is a letter to people caught in the crunch between two cultures. As people born into the Jewish faith, they were hated by the Gentiles. But as converts to Christianity, they were despised even more by their family for leaving their spiritual roots. Some were about to junk their newfound faith and return to Judaism when this letter was sent to them. As it circulated among them, it proved to be what was needed most. Today we call that letter the book of Hebrews.

You may be asking, "Why did Hebrews make such a difference?" The answer is found in the theme of the book: Jesus is superior; therefore He is our Savior.

The thread of the superiority of Jesus will be woven through the fabric of this study. Repeatedly we will see how this truth was riveted into the thinking of the first readers of this great letter. As it sustained them in tough times and gave them a greater love for Christ, so it will strengthen us and give us a deeper passion to walk with Jesus.

IT'S YOUR TURN

1. According to the following passages, how is Jesus superior?

   a. To the prophets (Hebrews 1:1-3)

   b. To the angels (1:4-6; 13; 2:7-8)

   c. To Moses (3:1-7)

d. To Joshua (4:8-16)

e. To the earthly priesthood (5:1-9)

f. To the Old Covenant (6:13-20)

g. To the Levitical law (7:25-27)

h. To the animal sacrifices (8:3-6; 9:11-15; 10:1-10)

2. Not only is Jesus superior to all of the above, but He gives us a superior way of living as we follow Him. Notice this as you glance through the following passages:

a. We have faith in God (Hebrews 11:1-6).

b. We have hope in Christ (12:1-3).

c. We have love for our brothers and sisters in Christ (13:17-18; 20-21).

THE FIRST
AND THE LAST WORD

In 1974 at Fulton County Stadium in Atlanta, Georgia, Hank Aaron broke the record set by Babe Ruth for the most home runs hit in professional baseball. As the ball sailed into the grandstands, the crowd lost control. For nearly 15 minutes they clapped and cheered as only those who had just witnessed a new world record being made could celebrate. The next day

7

every newspaper in America, and many around the world, carried the story with a bold "715!" emblazoned across the front page. Aaron still holds that record and is known as "the last word of baseball."

While Hank Aaron deserves recognition for his accomplishments as an athlete, only Jesus hit a grand slam against sin and sent the devil to the locker room with his tail between his legs. Only Jesus has the rightful title of being the First and the Last Word from God. This section of Hebrews endorses Him as the only One worthy of worship and celebration because of His position. The newspapers may not feature Him as such on the front page, but the Word of God which lasts forever proudly announces Him as King of kings and Lord of lords. This is the reason that He is superior to all!

IT'S YOUR TURN

1. Hebrews 1:1 mentions how God has spoken to our forefathers through the prophets. Who are some of these prophets?

2. The verse says God spoke through prophets in many times and in various ways. From

what you know of the Bible, list some of these.

TIMES   WAYS

3. Describe what you think it means to be an heir.

4. How do you see that Colossians 1:16-17 connects with Hebrews 1:2b?

5. If Jesus made the universe, what does that say about you?

6. Define the following words:

a. radiance

b. representation

c. sustaining

d. purification

How do these apply to Christ according to 1:3?

7. While we do not know how many angels there are, the Bible gives reference to three specific angels. Who are they? (See Isaiah 14:12 [KJV], Jude 9 and Luke 1:19 if you're stumped)

8. According to Hebrews 1:4-6, which angel has a name greater than Christ?

9. The writer of Hebrews talks about Jesus being superior with the opening of 1:8: "But about the Son, he says . . ." What does the writer say about Jesus in 1:8-12?

His throne will _ _ _ _   _ _ _   _ _ _ _   _ _ _
_ _ _ _ (1:8).

He has _ _ _ _ _ righteousness but hated
_ _ _ _ _ _ _ _ _ _ (1:9).

God has set Him above
_ _ _   _ _ _ _ _ _ _ _ _ _ (1:9).

His anointing is with oil of _ _ _ (1:9).

He _ _ _ _   _ _ _   _ _ _ _ _ _ _ _ _ _ of the
earth (1:10).

He will _ _ _ _ _ _ the same and His years
_ _ _ _   _ _ _ _ _ (1:12) end.

10. How could angels serve those who inher-
ited salvation? (See 1:14)

DON'T DRIFT OFF THE DIVINE COURSE

Any boat can drift off course or away from shore. A compass can fail or an anchor can lose its grip. From there even the smallest wind or current can take the craft into danger.

The same is true for the Christian. Neglecting spiritual disciplines will soon cause us to get off course. Spiritual compasses give security and keep us off coral reefs—and they keep us from becoming shipwrecked.

IT'S YOUR TURN

1. Have you ever met someone who became spiritually shipwrecked? What happened?

2. What are some spiritual anchors or compasses in your life?

3. What does this mean: "We must pay more careful attention, therefore, to what we have heard, so that we do not drift away"?

4. The writer speaks about the angels speaking a message. What is that referring to? (See Deuteronomy 33:2-4, Acts 7:38.) Why would it be binding?

5. Is there an escape for ignoring or drifting from our great salvation?

6. Who first announced salvation? Who affirmed it?

7. What does the writer mean by "signs, wonders and various miracles, and gifts of the Holy Spirit"? Check through the second and third chapters of Acts for some examples.

8. What do they have to do with our salvation?

9. How can these keep us from drifting off course?

WHY WE CAN NEVER BE ASHAMED OF JESUS

Have you ever been ashamed of being a friend to someone? There are times when admitting you know someone can be embarrassing. This is especially true if your friend does stupid things—like wearing clashing clothes, trying to get a date with your older sister (or younger brother) or scoring a point for the opposite team just to see if the coach would care. At times like that, wouldn't it be nice to be able to say, "Shut up," "Grow up" or maybe even, "You make me want to throw up!"?

In this passage, the writer of Hebrews points out several reasons why we can never be ashamed of Jesus. First of all, Jesus doesn't do stupid stuff. Second, not only is He our superior Savior, but He also is our best Friend.

IT'S YOUR TURN

1. Why do you think Hebrews 2:6 says, "What is man that you are mindful of him"?

2. Have you ever wanted to wear a real crown—and experience all that goes with it? What does 2:7 mean when it says "you crowned him with glory and honor"?

3. Why do you suppose God put everything under man's authority?

4. What caused that to cease?

5. According to 2:9, Jesus as a man (but not as God) was made a little lower than the angels. What does that tell you about Him coming to earth to be one of us?

6. Jesus is called the Author of our salvation. Why?

7. What does He call those who receive His salvation?

8. What did Jesus' death do to the devil's slave trade? (See 2:14-15)

9. Here we read that Jesus is merciful and faithful. Why would the writer say that?

10. Memorize Hebrews 2:18.

OUR SAVIOR—
SUPREME OVER ALL

So far the theme of Hebrews has been that Jesus is the Supreme One over (1) the prophets (2) the angels (3) death (4) the devil and (5) temptations. In Hebrews 3, this same proclamation is given, pointing out how Jesus is supreme over Moses. That must have been a shock to these Jewish people, for they had been taught no one could have been closer to God than Moses. Yet this part of Hebrews claims Jesus is supreme.

IT'S YOUR TURN

1. What would be some reasons that Jews would hold Moses in such high esteem?

2. Do you think of yourself as a holy brother or

19

sister? Do you see yourself as one with a "heavenly calling"? How do you respond to these descriptions of believers in Hebrews 3:1?

3. In 3:2, what single word is used to describe Moses and Jesus? What does that mean?

4. Why would Jesus be given a greater honor than Moses?

5. Hebrews 3:4-6 discusses a house being built. What role would Moses play in that construction job?

__Master builder   __Foreman   __Laborer

__Ditch digger   __Architect

__Blueprint pressman

6. What role would Jesus play?

  __Master builder   __Foreman   __Laborer

  __Ditch digger   __Architect

  __Blueprint pressman

7. Why are we called God's house? How does that fit with First Corinthians 6:19-20?

8. How can we remain God's house? (See John 15:1-5)

9. Since we are an example of God's house, who lives in us? (See John 14:15-17)

10. What does that tell us when we are sad? Happy? Lonely? Depressed? Filled with pain? Angry? Facing death? Filled with the joy of the Lord?

NEEDED: A HEART THAT PUMPS FOR GOD

THUMP THUMP THUMP

Health clinics, gyms, jazzercise, aerobics and warm-ups. These are household terms in our culture today. More people are exercising today than ever in history. The reason is clear: the healthier your heart is, the greater the chances that you will live longer. Wanting good health has convinced people to stop smoking, lay off the junk food and follow a low-fat, high-fiber diet.

Eating oat bran today is better than choking down heart pills tomorrow!

In this passage we find a warning issued about caring for another kind of heart—our spiritual hearts. The message is clear: don't let your spiritual heart become hardened. The reason for the warning is simple—a spiritually calcified heart doesn't have a place for Christ. Therefore, the call is for us to have a heart pumping for God!

IT'S YOUR TURN

1. When was the last time you had a spiritual heart exam?

2. What contrasts can be noted in the following?

   3:12 _____, unbelieving heart vs. living _____

   3:12-13 unbelieving _____ vs. _____ one another

   3:13-14 sin's _____vs. _____ firmly to the end

3:14-15 _____ your hearts vs.
_____ in Christ

3:14-15 as you did in the _____
vs. the _____ we had at first

3. Why is rebellion a major cause of spiritual hardheartedness?

4. What caused God to become angry at Israel? How long were they in the desert?

5. List some of the things we can practice daily to keep our spiritual hearts soft and pumping strong for God.

6. What should happen if we decide not to have a pliable heart?

7. Have you ever known someone who made that choice? What happened?

8. Rest is something we all need to keep us in good health. Verse 19 says that because of their disobedience and hardheartedness, God denied the Israelites rest. If that is the negative side of God's bargain, what is the positive side?

GOD'S DEFINITION OF "R&R"

What do you think of when you think of "R&R"? For some, that stands for "Rock & Roll." But for most people "R&R" stands for "rest & relaxation." "Rest & relaxation" is often described as soaking up the rays at the beach or sleeping until noon and then eating lunch just before an afternoon snooze. How do *you* define "R&R"? Better yet, how do you suppose *God* defines "R&R"? Let's look into this passage and discover for ourselves.

IT'S YOUR TURN

1. How do you spend your "R&R" time?

2. By looking at 4:1-2, how would you say God defines "R&R"?

27

3. What role does faith in Christ play in spiritual "R&R"?

4. How important is rest to God according to 4:4?

5. Why did God say that Israel would not enter rest?

6. If we refuse to believe in Christ and place our confidence in Him, why can we never experience spiritual "R&R"?

7. How could pride keep you from experiencing God's rest?

8. Have you ever experienced total rest? Or are you panicked that God's plan won't work for you?

9. List some of the habits that could keep someone from receiving God's peace and keep them from having spiritual "R&R."

SCRIPTURAL SURGERY

$\mathcal{S}$urgery is never fun. Often fear grips those who are facing surgery: Will something go wrong? Will someone make a mistake? How bad will the pain that follows be? While surgery is never pleasant, it does correct problems and is part of a process that can offer a better life.

In a real sense, this is what scriptural surgery can be like. When God begins operating on our spiritual heart, He cuts deeply, exposing the sin we have hidden in there. Often that is painful. It can even be embarrassing. We wonder if God still loves us and has good plans for us. However, just as surgery corrects physical problems, so scriptural surgery mends and repairs spiritual problems. Our comfort zone may get squeezed, but in the end our walk with Christ will be enhanced.

IT'S YOUR TURN

1. Have you ever faced surgery? If so, what were your feelings?

2. How has God performed scriptural surgery on you in the last six months?

3. Is it hard to admit to problems in your life?

4. Are you fighting God about a scriptural surgery that is needed in your life right now?

5. List the three descriptions that are given in the passage concerning the Word of God.

a.

b.

c.

6. How would you define these phrases?

a.

b.

c.

7. According to this passage, how much is hidden from God?

8. We need to grasp the truth that God wants to correct spiritual problems in our lives because He loves us. How does this affect your attitude toward God's "surgery"?

9. Are you afraid of allowing God to cut into your spiritual heart? Are you afraid He will expose something sinful in you and then say, "You're too disgusting and sinful for me to love any longer!"? If so, why?

10. Can you trust God to remove the junk in your life? Do you believe He wants only the best for you? Pray now and ask the Lord to show you His plan for your spiritual life.

STUDY 9

HEBREWS 4:14-5:10

A REFEREE WHO NEVER MAKES A BAD CALL

In basketball, no one on the court is as important as the referee. Though he may be two feet shorter than anyone else in the entire gym, he is the one who tells the 7'3" players who's right and who's wrong! The sound of his whistle stops all activity and athletes who make millions of dollars can be sent up to the foul line for a free shot or out of the game for violating the rules. There is no coach, owner or fan in the world who can exercise more authority than the guy in the black and white stripes. His call is the last word!

Just as a ref has the final call in a basketball game, so Jesus has the final call in life. No one has greater authority or power than He does. His calls are always accurate. No matter what protest may be given, what He says goes. As God's Son, He alone is given that title, and no one else can share it. He alone is our Great High Priest.

IT'S YOUR TURN

1. Have you ever seen a referee make a bad call? What happened?

2. How does it make you feel when you read that Jesus, as our priest before God, *never* makes a bad call?

3. Describe some ways that Jesus was tempted as we are today.

4. Because Jesus never sinned, what do we have that enables us to approach God's throne?

5. What are some of the roles a priest played in the life of the people in Old Testament times? (See Exodus 28:29-30; 29:4-9, 44-46; Leviticus 9:22-24)

6. According to Hebrews 5:4, who could be a priest? Why?

7. How do Hebrews 4:15 and 5:7-10 fit together?

8. From what you know of Jesus' life, what were some ways He learned to submit?

9. How can we be sure that Jesus will never make a bad call the way some referees do?

10. Since Jesus is our Great High Priest, how can we hold onto the faith that we profess? (See 4:16)

HEBREWS 5:11-6:3

SPIRITUAL BULIMIA WON'T WORK

A major problem that affects many American teens today is eating disorders. When people suffer from eating disorders, they are affected not only physically, but mentally as well. Malnutrition can quickly cause emotional as well as physical difficulties that can be overcome only by a disciplined, balanced diet.

The same dietary principles that work for us physically are also true spiritually. We must be nourished in a steady, consistent way that meets our individual needs. We can't grow by just grabbing a spiritual bite here and there. To do so does nothing more for us than snacking on spiritual "junk food." Neither can we just show up at church and gorge ourselves on Sunday, only to starve ourselves the rest of the week. That is spiritual bulimia—*not* a way to grow in Christ. The answer is a consistent diet of the Word.

IT'S YOUR TURN

1. Why do so many teens today have such poor eating habits?

2. Below is a list of foods. Put in order what a child should be given from the time he/she is a newborn until kindergarten.

   __steak   __potato chips   __bananas
   __milk   __baby food   __hot sauce
   __"crushed veggies"   __BBQ chicken

3. How long have you been a Christian? According to the food groups above, what should you be able to digest spiritually?

4. Circle what your spiritual diet is most of the time.

   crackers   "crushed veggies"

   milk   meat of the Word

5. How important is a variety of spiritual food?

6. How often do you eat spiritually?

__once a week   __three times a week
__twice a week   __daily

7. Who does your "spiritual cooking"?

__pastor   __no one; I don't eat
__youth pastor   __I cook for myself
__other   __friend

8. Why do you suppose the people receiving this letter were "slow to learn"?

9. Why does a baby not know that not everything is supposed to go in its mouth? Why do baby Christians put just anything in their spiritual bowls and eat it?

HEBREWS 6:4-12

THE ENERGY OF ENCOURAGEMENT

Encouragement is one of the most powerful resources known to mankind. People the world over would prefer kind words to harsh ones every time. This was proven in an experiment secretly conducted in a classroom. When the teacher told her students to sit down more often and gave the commands in harsh tones, the students stood up longer and more often. However, when the same teacher told the same students how much she appreciated their good behavior, the students' had to be corrected 33 percent less often than they were when the teacher used harsh words.

In this passage, the writer of Hebrews is encouraging the readers to not fall away from serving God 110 percent. This section is dealing with repentance (6:6) and bad crops (6:7). The same message applies to us today. If we choose to abide in Christ, we will produce good crops within us and will not need to repent for deserting the Lord's ways. Just as the Hebrews were encouraged by what is found in 6:11, so we can be energized with this message today: "show this same diligence to the very end, in order to make your hope sure."

IT'S YOUR TURN

1. What is the most encouraging thing that has ever happened to you? How did it change you?

2. Name three ways Hebrews 6:4-12 encourages you.

   a.

   b.

   c.

3. How does Hebrews 6:4-6 encourage believers to repent?

4. What do repenting and a piece of land with thorns and thistles have in common?

5. Why does fire cleanse the land of thorns and thistles? How does that apply to the believer according to John 15:1-5?

6. How does the writer compliment his readers in Hebrews 6:9?

7. How can we say that God is not unjust and doesn't forget our work?

8. Name some ways that people are energized when others help them. How can you help someone this week?

9. What will other Christians who serve God patiently receive as an inheritance?

FATHER ABRAHAM MAY HAVE HAD MANY SONS . . . BUT HE SURE DIDN'T HAVE MANY DOUBTS!

If you ever attended a VBS, children's church, camp or Sunday school, you probably sang the little chorus called "Father Abraham." You will recall the leg and arm motions and head nods required of everyone as they sang. (It's a wonder more people don't get knocked out during this song!)

In this concluding section of Hebrews 6, the writer gives an illustration of how believers can be encouraged in their walk with God. Using Abraham as an example, we see that despite waiting for over 24 years, Abraham stayed true to God, who had promised him a son. The result is that doubts never overcame him, and God did exactly as He had promised. With that as our hope, we too can overcome discouragement and doubts.

IT'S YOUR TURN

1. Have you ever wondered why people go through hard times?

2. What has caused you to doubt your relationship with God?

3. If you ever stopped trusting God, what would your life be like?

4. Why do you suppose the writer of Hebrews put this illustration of Abraham in this section?

5. Do you think Abraham ever questioned God about the promises made to him? Why did God promise Abraham anything at all? (See Romans 4:18-21)

6. How hard is it for you to live out Hebrews 6:15 and to wait patiently?

7. What is the key description of God found in Hebrews 6:17?

8. Why did God make good on his promise to Abraham? (See 6:18) What two things are unchangeable about God?

9. According to Hebrews 6:19, what does this do for us?

10. What role did Jesus play on our behalf so that the promises of God could be extended to us? What does that do for us when doubts come?

A TOUGH PASSAGE WITH A TENDER MESSAGE

*S*ometimes words have to be heard in their context before their meaning can be understood.

Example #1: **Killer!**

Killer could identify a type of whale, refer to a murderer or describe a hard test at school.

Example #2: **Sweet!**

This could describe something you tasted, something you enjoyed seeing ("That soccer goal from 60 yards out was *sweet!*") or someone nice ("She is so sweet!").

The same is true of Hebrews 7. This is a hard passage to grasp until we understand the comparison between Christ and the other priests. Chuck Swindoll gives us an outline to help us understand this section of Scripture.

ALL OTHER PRIESTS

1. There was no oath from God that established them as priests. All that entitled them to the office was their physical tie to the tribe of Levi (v. 20).

2. Under the Old Covenant a guarantee was lacking.

3. The ministry of human priests was temporary; death prevented them from continuing (v. 23).

JESUS

1. Jesus' priesthood was established with an oath from God Himself (v. 21); see also Psalm 110, especially verse 4.

2. Under the New Covenant Jesus Himself is the guarantee (v. 22).

3. The ministry of Jesus' priesthood is permanent; He "abides forever" (v. 24) and "always lives to intercede for them" (v. 25).

from *The Preeminent Person of Christ, A Study of Hebrews 1-10*, 125. Charles R. Swindoll. Fullerton, CA: Insight for Living, 1989.

IT'S YOUR TURN

1. According to this chapter, who was Melchizedek?

2. In Hebrews 7:7, Melchizedek is declared to be greater than Abraham. Why would that be so if Abraham had the promises of God?

3. Jesus became the guarantee of a better covenant. How is that covenant better? What is it that Jesus guarantees? (See 7:22-25)

4. Explain in your own words how Jesus is superior to all other priests in the Old Testament.

5. Three reasons for Jesus' superiority are cited in Hebrews 7:26-28. List them.

   a. 7:26

   b. 7:27

   c. 7:28

6. How could the teaching of Hebrews 7 encourage the people who had left Judaism to follow Christ? How would it help those who were hated by the Gentiles?

7. How would you connect John 14:6-7 to Hebrews 7?

8. The goal of many religions is to know God and to meet the standards to be in His presence. How does Hebrews 7 fulfill that quest?

A NEW COVENANT— THAT'S ALWAYS NEW!

Getting anything new is always thrilling. To have the newest car, the latest style of clothes, most recent stereo component or the newest PC is always exciting—but there is one problem. New eventually becomes old.

There is one thing, though, that will always be new, and that is the New Covenant. In this portion of Hebrews the writer continues to point out how Christ is superior, for He alone made a covenant that never becomes obsolete or in need of repair. According to Scripture, it is always new! What an awesome God we have!

IT'S YOUR TURN

1. What is the newest thing you own? How long will you consider it new?

2. How would you connect Hebrews 8:1 with Hebrews 8:6?

3. Why would the writer talk about the "true" tabernacle to the Jewish Christians who first received this letter?

4. Why do you think that Jesus *sat down* in heaven? What is significant about the act of sitting down?

5. Why did God promise a New Covenant? How is it superior to the old one? (See verse 6)

6. How is the New Covenant different from the old law regarding inner peace and external "works"?

7. How does the New Covenant offer a close relationship with God, whereas the old law kept people at a distance from God?

8. Scan Second Corinthians 5:7-17 and then re-read Hebrews 8. Jot down some contrasts that you may find.

LIFE BEFORE CHRIST

LIFE SINCE YOU MET CHRIST

STUDY 15

HEBREWS 9:1-14

WHEN A TENT WAS REPLACED BY A MANSION

Imagine camping in the desert for two weeks. There would be little to do except pray for shade, avoid cacti and slap sand fleas. After 14 grueling days of this misery, you then check into the finest hotel you have ever seen. The climate is controlled, the carpet under your feet is soft and there isn't a bug in the whole joint. You are comfortable, at peace and able to relax, knowing the bill is paid in full.

In essence, the difference between sleeping in a tent amidst the blazing heat of the desert and checking into a four-star hotel is the difference between the Old Testament law and tabernacle and the finished work of Christ in the New Testament. No longer is fear a part of one's relationship with God. People are now able to relax, fully confident that Christ has totally paid the bill for sin. Peace is now ushered in where once only anxiety ruled. The "tent" of sacrifice was replaced by a mansion where all who wish to come in from the desert are welcome.

IT'S YOUR TURN

1. Does your conscience ever nag you about your old sins? What do 9:14 and 15 tell you about freedom from the bondage of sin?

2. The verses in this section speak of the contest between the Old Testament tabernacle and the hope Christ offers. As you scan this section and the verses around it, find the differences between these two covenants.

TABERNACLE OF O.T.

a. Endless

_ _ _ _ _ _ _ _ _ _

b. (9:13-14) _ _ _ _ _ of animals

c. (9:9-10, 12, 14)

_ _ _ _ _ _ _ _ _
payment for sin

d. Only for _ _ _ _ _ _

e. (9:3, 24) Completed in _ _ _ _ _ _ _ _

_ _ _ _ _

f. (9:13-14)

_ _ _ _ _ _ _
cleansing

g. (9:10, 15) External

_ _ _ _ _ _ _ _ _ _ _

NEW COVENANT OF N.T.

a. One   _ _ _ _ _ _ _ _
_

b. _ _ _ _ _ of Christ

c. _ _ _ _ _   payment for sin

d. For _ _ _ _ _ _ who believes

e. Completed in

_ _ _ _ _ _

f. _ _ _ _ _ _
cleansing

g. Set _ _ _ _

THE BLESSING OF SALVATION COMES FROM THE BLOOD OF OUR SAVIOR

E ach year the Red Cross comes to nearly every community in America for a blood drive. People are encouraged to give a pint of blood to replenish the local supply needed for surgeries and transfusions. Without blood, we cannot live. People who give blood give life to those who couldn't live without it.

Hebrews 9:22 says, "In fact, the law requires that nearly everything be cleansed with blood, and without the shedding of blood there is no forgiveness." As we need blood physically, so we need blood spiritually. By giving His blood as a sacrifice in place of ours, our Lord Jesus Christ brings us salvation—spiritual life.

IT'S YOUR TURN

1. Have you ever given blood for a blood drive? Have you or has anyone you know needed blood for surgery or in an emergency?

2. What kind of inheritance is promised to those who are under the New Covenant founded on Christ's sacrifice?

3. Why do you suppose Christ made a "will" (New Covenant) while He was living? (See Hebrews 9:16-17) Who benefits from His "will"?

4. According to the Old Testament law given to Moses, how necessary was the shedding of blood for sin to be forgiven?

5. How does that apply to Christ in the New Testament covenant?

6. How can we be sure that Christ's suffering and the shedding of His blood was enough to forgive us and make a way for us?

7. God's Word tells us we must face two things—death and judgment. How does that affect you in the here and now?

8. What does the final work of Christ have to do with His return?

9. What role does the Holy Spirit play in com-
municating to mankind about the blessing of
salvation found in the blood of Jesus?

ASSURANCE, ATONEMENT AND A RELATIONSHIP— IF WE STAY WITH JESUS

All through the book of Hebrews the writer reminds his readers that Jesus is superior to any other religion or system known to man. Christ alone is greater than any prophet, priest, king or philosophy.

The writer encourages the readers to stay true to Jesus, for if they do, they will have an assurance that their sin is atoned for and God is walking with them. However, there are severe consequences for not staying true to Christ.

The warning is honest: we have hope when we have Christ, but without Him, we lose every time.

IT'S YOUR TURN

1. What does your relationship with God mean to you? Why?

2. Define the phrase "new and living way" used in Hebrews 10:20.

3. How can we draw near to God and have a holy relationship with Him without fear? What can we do if our conscience is not clear? Can we still draw near? Why?

4. How can you encourage someone to hold onto God's way and keep moving toward love and good deeds?

5. What "Day" is the writer referring to in Hebrews 10:25?

6. According to Hebrews 10:26-27, what will be the outcome for those who reject God's way?

7. Explain the correlation between the illustration of what happened to those who rejected God's law in Moses' day and those who treat the blood of Jesus with disdain.

8. How does the writer remind his readers of the price they have already paid for following Christ? (See Hebrews 10:32-34)

9. What encourages you most in Hebrews 10:35-36?

10. Are you shrinking back from following Christ? If so, how does this passage speak to you? If not, how can you use this to encourage others from falling away?

THE HALL OF FAITH

There are halls of fame all over America. These halls of fame give tribute to people who have set records or made significant contributions in their fields. Athletic halls of fame usually feature pictures or memorabilia highlighting an athlete's career. At colleges, the "halls of fame" are buildings named after important people who gave large contributions to the college in some way.

In Hebrews 11, there is a tribute that could be called the "Hall of Faith." Hebrews 1-10 reiterates the superiority of Christ. Hebrews 11 is like walking down a hallway of pictures of those who by faith chose to go God's way at any cost. Because of their faithfulness to God, our faith is strengthened when we make the same choice.

IT'S YOUR TURN

1. How would you define faith? How does Hebrews 11:1 define it?

2. Do you know someone who has shown great faith in Jesus? How did this person show faith?

3. This passage mentions Gideon, Barak, Samson and Jephthah (11:32). If you're not familiar with their exploits, read Judges 4:6-5:15, 6:11-8:35, 11:1-12:7 and 13:1-16:31.

4. Make a list of all the people mentioned in Hebrews 11. Beside each name, write what he or she is known for.

PERSON   **DEED OF FAITH**

5. Verses 39 and 40 say that these faithful people didn't receive what was promised but would get something better along with us. When do you think we will receive this promise?

6. Ask God to increase your faith and to make you the caliber of person that these people mentioned in Hebrews 11 were. Who knows—maybe someday you will be in the "Hall of Faith" of the upcoming generation!

DIVINE DISCIPLINE

What comes to your mind when you hear the word "discipline"? Standing in the corner? Spankings? Being grounded? No phone for two weeks? You probably link the "d" word with punishment.

In this portion of Scripture, however, "discipline" is associated with staying focused to accomplish a set goal. Even as a runner must stay focused on the finish line to win the race, so people who are in spiritual training must remain intent and disciplined to finish the race of holiness. A runner doesn't just jog around on the track, waving at the fans in the bleachers. Instead there is a passion within that removes all distractions. We are not called to "stroll" with the Lord, but to excel and to have everything within us ignite as we submit to God's discipline. The cost of discipleship isn't cheap. Neither was the cross. What is your choice?

IT'S YOUR TURN

1. What is the first mental image you have when you hear the word "discipline"?

2. Describe the difference between discipline as punishment and discipline as training.

3. How does the "Hall of Faith" in Hebrews 11 connect with Hebrews 12:1?

4. There are many people listed in Hebrews 11. Name three that are key examples to you and state why their discipline is a model for you to follow.

NAME   REASON

   a.

   b.

   c.

5. How did Jesus remain disciplined while He ran the race of holiness when He was on earth?

6. Hebrews 1-10 points out how Jesus is superior to any other religion or philosophy. Hebrews 11 is about those who responded to the Lord's discipline and stayed true to God. How do these two divisions within the book of Hebrews serve to motivate you to "throw off everything that hinders" and stay true to God?

7. How would you say that the Lord's love is seen in the way He disciplines His children?

8. Why is it that people have respect for those who exercise discipline, but lack appreciation for those who don't?

9. Give an example of how Hebrews 12:11 has been a part of your life.

10. What could be classified as a "feeble arm" or "weak knees" in your spiritual life? How could discipline and focus strengthen them?

GOD'S MEGAPHONE TO MANKIND

It is amazing how you can make your voice louder simply by cupping your hands around your mouth as you speak. You can increase the distance your voice normally travels and point your words in a certain direction. You can project your voice even more when you use a megaphone. Though a cheerleader may weigh only 90 pounds, using a megaphone allows her to make her voice louder than the noise that comes from several hundred people cheering in the grandstand!

In our last lesson we saw we are called to run in a race, submitting to the Lord's discipline. This race is not conducted on some little field where just anyone can strap on their sneakers and enjoy a few laps around the track. This is a race for holiness, where only those in Christ have the stuff to run.

In this passage, it is as though God has a megaphone. With a commanding voice that is projected above the devil's crowd, He is saying to all the runners, "Remember My ways! Stay true to the holy things. I will meet you at the finish line, and there I will share with you the reality of My unshakable kingdom."

Do you hear God encouraging you along the track? Keep running in His might.

IT'S YOUR TURN

1. Explain in your own words how holiness is a must if we are to run the race described in Hebrews 12.

2. How could a bitter spirit affect a runner in the race of holiness? What do you think God

would be saying into the megaphone about bitterness?

3. What do the terms "sexual immorality" and "godlessness" mean? Why would these disqualify someone from this race?

4. In Hebrews 12:18-21 the writer mentions the terror that those in Moses' day felt toward God. Hebrews 12:22-24 speaks of assurance for those who are in Christ. Why the difference?

5. Describe what you believe God would say to a runner who is considering dropping out of the race.

6. What is it that cannot be shaken according to Hebrews 12:27-28?

7. Whose commanding voice are you hearing these days—God's voice or the world's? Why? Do you think both want to say something to you? What would be the difference in the message?

8. What are you most thankful for since you became a member of God's track team?

9. Describe what you believe is acceptable, reverent worship of God. Use the teaching of Hebrews to support your ideas.

10. Why is God described as a consuming fire? What fuels this fire? What can withstand the heat generated from this fire?

STUDY 21

HEBREWS 13

PUTTING HEBREWS INTO ACTION (PART 1)

F ew things are more frustrating than to have something that doesn't work. Having the fastest car in town doesn't mean a thing if it's sitting in your driveway with the battery missing. Owning an incredible stereo is worthless if the wires are disconnected. The same thing is true about our faith. If it doesn't work and produce a difference within us towards others and God, it is useless!

Fortunately, Hebrews 13 is a practical "wrap up" to the teaching of the rest of the book. This chapter teaches us how to relate to others, to God and to the things of this world. It ties the teaching of the book to a basic "nuts-and-bolts," everyday living for God.

IT'S YOUR TURN

1. How should a disciple today relate to others?

2. According to Hebrews 13:1, we should keep on loving each other as brothers. Describe how the unconditional love of Christ could motivate us to give unconditional love to brothers who are "geeks"—or just weird.

3. What does God say about efforts to love others who are not the same as you are? (See Hebrews 13:16, 25.)

4. In a day where crime is on the increase, why do you suppose God would tell us to not forget to entertain strangers? (See Hebrews 13:2)

5. Have you ever met someone who believes he or she has encountered an angel? Do you think *you* may have encountered an angel? What happened?

6. Think of some other kinds of prisons besides ones with bars and locks on the doors. Why should we care for people in jail and in these other situations?

7. Why would words on marriage be in a chapter on relationships? What does Hebrews 13:4 say about marriage? What does it say about adultery? Immorality? How does that relate to the superiority of Christ?

8. Hebrews 13:5b-6 speaks of the relationship between a disciple and the Lord. Describe the hope found in these verses.

9. According to Hebrews 13:8 and 15, what confidence can we have because of Christ?

10. How would you apply the prayer in Hebrews 13:20-21 to your life?

PUTTING HEBREWS INTO ACTION (PART 2)

In the last study we saw how we are to relate to brothers, strangers, angels, prisoners, marriage partners and the Lord. Hebrews 13 is a "user-friendly" chapter. It centers on relationships in this life, giving clear guidelines on how to implement the difference Jesus makes in our lives in everyday living. Read through the chapter again quickly to refresh your memory.

IT'S YOUR TURN

1. Hebrews 13:7 talks about leaders. Why should we pay attention to leaders instead of just living independently?

2. How do you suppose God would have us relate to leaders who are nothing more than "control freaks"?

3. How difficult is it for you to submit to godly leaders? What does the teaching in Hebrews 13:17 say about that?

4. Hebrews was written to people who were suffering for their faith in Christ. Some were considering recanting their profession of faith and going back to their old ways. How can we encourage people going through hard times today because of their faith in Christ? (See Hebrews 13:18-19)

5. Why do you suppose the writer of Hebrews asks for prayer? Wouldn't you think the writer would be "spiritual enough"?

6. What does the request for prayer by the writer of Hebrews tell you about the Body of Christ? Leaders? People who are suffering?

7. According to Hebrews 13:5a, what role should money play in our lives? How can we practice what this verse says?

8. Hebrews 13:9-14 talks about worship practices. How can we guard ourselves against strange teachings? How are we strengthened in our hearts as we worship?

9. How do you suppose Hebrews 13:11-13 ties into our lives today? Have you ever met anyone who has suffered for the cause of Christ? What happened?

10. Because of our relationship with Jesus, we

have a promise of a city that is to come (Hebrews 13:14). How does that connect with what Jesus said in John 14:1-5? How does that fit with Philippians 3:20? Ephesians 2:19?

INTRODUCTION: THE ABC'S ABOUT THE AUTHOR

First Peter is not a warm and fuzzy collection of inspirational phrases. It is not written to weak-hearted wimps who sniffle their way through life, hoping someone will hand them a tissue. This book calls for disciples to stand up, square their shoulders, hold their heads high and receive the grace and guts it takes to live for God in a hostile world.

If there was one disciple who knew about having grace and guts, it was Peter. No other disciple is mentioned so often in Scripture, spoke so much for the group, was reproved more often by Jesus or received as much praise from the Lord as Peter. No other disciple was as exciting or life-like as Peter. Let's take a closer look at this deep-sea fisherman who became a disciple by using the first four letters of the alphabet.

Acknowledgement—In Matthew 16:16 Peter acknowledged Jesus to be "the Christ, the Son of the living God!" In response, Jesus said He would build His church on this confession and the gates of hell would not be able to stand against it!

Boldness—While Peter did not always bat a thousand, he was always willing to step up to the plate. Because of his boldness, God used him to preach the first sermon at Pentecost, and 3,000 people resigned from the devil's team and joined God's.

Christ-centered—Peter had a way of pointing people to Christ. He modeled Christianity when he preached, discipled others, led the church in its earliest days, and even when he failed.

Denial—Peter is also known for his denying Christ three times in just a few minutes. That would have been enough to knock most people out of the game. Yet because of Peter's repentant heart, Jesus put him up to bat again. With the fresh dose of grace and guts, Peter ripped a grand slam right over the devil's head.

IT'S YOUR TURN

1. Would you consider yourself a wimp or a warrior as a disciple? Why?

2. How has God given you grace?

3. In what areas do you need grace and guts to live for God?

4. Where do you identify most with Peter?

5. Would your closest friends agree that you confess Jesus to be "the Son of the living God"? Why or why not?

6. Peter was bold. Are you? How could the Lord make you more so?

7. On a scale of 1-10, where are you in being Christlike?

Not Christlike   An "OK" disciple   Christlike
  1 2 3   4 5 6   8 9 10

8. Peter denied the Lord three times. Have you ever denied Him?

9. Peter later repented. Have you ever done that? What did God do as a result?

WHAT TO DO WITH YOUR TEETH IN TOUGH TIMES

No two people are alike. Our looks, clothes and thoughts are different. So are our tastes, music preferences and skills. We each have our own views on politics, religion and how to celebrate holidays.

There is one thing that we all have in common. We all need something to sink our teeth into when we go through tough times. I'm not talking about our pearly whites, but rather our emotions. When we struggle in life because of emotional pain, we need something to stabilize us. Peter writes in this section of Scripture that no Christian is exempt from getting kicked in the teeth emotionally. When we begin to understand and live out the truth that despite the tough times, God will be there for us, our faith increases. As we do that, we receive the grace and guts to live for God! And that will not spoil or fade.

IT'S YOUR TURN

1. Peter wrote to people going through tough times. Have you been through a tough time lately? Describe it.

2. Check off what will perish, spoil or fade:

    __pizza   __new car   __latest CD
    __relationships   __prayer
    __money   __your body   __Bible

3. How can we rejoice in suffering grief in all kinds of trials?

4. What is the most painful emotional "kick in the teeth" you have ever experienced?

5. What six things are listed in 1:3-9 that are the result of our faith?

   a. 1:3—He has given us _ _ _   _ _ _ _ _

   b. 1:4—an _ _ _ _ _ _ _ _ _ _ _ that will never perish

   c. 1:5—through _ _ _ _ _ we are shielded by God's power

   d. 1:6—in this you can _ _ _ _ _ _ _
   _ _ _ _ _ _ _

   e. 1:8—you believe in him and have
   _ _ _ _ _ _ _ _ _ _ _ _ _ and _ _ _ _ _ _ _ _
   joy

   f. 1:9—the goal of your faith, the
   _ _ _ _ _ _ _ _ _ of your _ _ _ _ _

6. Why do you suppose Peter said our faith is more precious than gold?

7. What benefit is there to being refined by tough times?

8. What will it be like for you when Jesus is revealed?

9. See if any of the following verses provide any "meat" for you to sink your teeth into when you go through tough times: Proverbs 3:5-6; Romans 5:3-4; John 16:33; James 1:2-4.

STUDY 25

1 PETER 1:13-21

STAYING CLEAN IN A FILTHY WORLD

People often wonder how they can stay spiritually clean in a sinful society. Many have become too frustrated and given up altogether. Others have decided to isolate themselves from people, fearing "contamination" from the world. But Peter writes a different message here in this passage. Instead of isolation he talks about insulation. Do you see the distinction? Isolation keeps you away from the world; insulation keeps you in it, but protected from it. When insulation is applied, the clean stuff stays in, and the filthy stuff stays out.

IT'S YOUR TURN

1. Have you ever wondered where you could go so that you could be away from sin?

2. Where do you think that would be, and how long would you want to stay there?

3. What do you think about Peter's idea of insulation? How does it fit in with First John 2:15-17?

4. What role do you think your mind should play in keeping you spiritually clean and morally pure?

5. What does Peter mean when he says that God is holy and we should be also? How can that be?

6. Scan through 1:13-21 and see if you can find listed any "disinfectants"—things that if applied would help keep you clean in a society full of garbage. Write them down as you find them.

7. How do you think Jesus kept himself spiritually clean?

__prayer   __He didn't   __fasting

__took authority over the devil

__being popular   __stayed focused

__let somebody else do it for Him

8. Why is obedience important?

9. What does God say about judgment in this passage? How does this fit in with these passages?

Psalm 1:5

Hebrews 10:10-18

Acts 10:42

Romans 14:10-12

STUDY 26

1 PETER 1:22-2:12

HANGIN' TOGETHER—IT'S A GOD-PEOPLE THING

In this section Peter is encouraging the disciples to care for one another. Unity in the Church is as important as it is on any team. This doesn't mean that unity equals uniformity, nor does oneness equal sameness. Being a disciple does not mean being stamped out by a cookie cutter where everyone talks thinks, acts, dresses and smells the same. Being a disciple is learning to think, act and react like Jesus. The goal for the Church is to love people and try to hang together through thick and thin.

IT'S YOUR TURN

1. Are there any people in your youth group or Bible study that are really different than you? Is that easy for you to accept?

2. Why do you think Jesus prayed the way He did in John 17:20-23?

3. How did Peter say we should purify ourselves?

4. In 1:23-25, Peter discusses the word of God, giving several descriptions as to what it's like. List some of these.

5. Part of learning to accept others is learning what might keep us from receiving them as Jesus would. According to 2:1, what does Peter say we should get rid of from our lives to help us be able to do that?

6. What does Peter mean by "pure spiritual milk"?

7. What does it mean to be part of a chosen people and a holy nation in Christ?

8. In the Old Testament a royal priest was a godly person who served the king. In the New Testament we are to be in godly service to another king. Who do you suppose Peter is implying that king is?

9. Why should we be aliens and strangers in this world? Do people see you as a native?

STUDY 27

1 PETER 2:13-25

UNDER
AUTHORITY—
THE WAY TO
STAY ON TOP!

In our culture we are taught that being in submission to anyone is about as attractive as gravy from your school cafeteria. Nearly every voice in our society—all the way from MTV and Madonna to politicians and *Cosmopolitan Magazine*—pounds us daily with the message that only the weak submit and obey.

Fortunately, we don't have to take our cues from people on MTV or anyone else who doesn't understand God's pattern of living. We get our call right from God's Book. According to it, we are on top when we are under submission!

IT'S YOUR TURN

1. What are some negative ideas we hear in our world about being in submission?

2. Who are some authorities in your life? Are you able to submit to them easily?

3. In Acts 4:1-20 Peter and John were told by the political leaders to stop preaching. They did not, and eventually went to jail for breaking the law. Why do you suppose Peter is writing now about submitting to authorities?

4. According to 2:15, what is God's will for you to do?

5. In what two specific ways does Peter tell us to live in 2:16?

   a.

   b.

6. What kind of example did Jesus leave for us in the area of submission? (See Isaiah 53, Philippians 2:5-11, Hebrews 5:7-10)

7. What does being in submission mean to you?

   __you're worthless   __no guts
   __Christlikeness   __courage
   __God's will   __spineless

8. Review the following passages concerning being in submission to authorities.

   Romans 13:1-5

   Ephesians 5:21-33

   Ephesians 6:1

   1 Timothy 2:11

   James 4:7

HOW TO HAVE MAGIC IN YOUR MARRIAGE

It would be the understatement of the century to say that marriages are in trouble in America. It is now more likely that a marriage will end in divorce than by the death of a spouse. The average lawn mower lasts longer (9.5 years) than the average marriage (5.5 years). It would take a stadium nine times the size of the Rose Bowl to hold all of the grandparents who are raising grandchildren whose parents are divorced.

Although marriage is probably not a high priority for you now, you can think about what you want your marriage to be like when you get there. Thankfully, we do not have to fall into America's current pattern. This passage teaches us that marriage can be all that God designed it to be. Following the prescription given in this passage will bring magic into marriage.

IT'S YOUR TURN

1. Why do you think so many marriages are ending in divorce today?

2. Why do you think Peter uses Sarah as an example for women to follow?

3. What are some "secrets" Peter shares with women who live with an unsaved husband?

4. Do you think there is anything wrong or immoral about braided hair, jewelry and attractive clothes? According to 3:3-4, where should beauty stem from?

5. What "magic" is brought into a marriage when a person practices a quiet, gentle spirit?

6. How important is it to have a good attitude in any relationship?

7. Peter tells the men to "live with your wives." In essence he is saying, "understand your wife" or "be close to her." Why do you suppose Peter said that to the men?

8. What does it mean to treat someone with respect?

9. How can a husband best demonstrate respect toward his wife?

__buy her jewelry   __ignore her
__talk about deep issues
__listen to her fears   __treat her kindly
__let her have 10 of his children

10. According to this teaching, what happens to the prayers of the man who doesn't show kindness or respect towards his wife?

HOW'S IT "GROWING"?

Sometimes when we talk to someone, we ask, "How's it going?" In this section, it is as though Peter is asking "how's it *growing*?" He is concerned about the relationship between the people and the Lord. Remember, Peter is writing to people who are facing hard times, and they need a lot of grace and guts to continue to serve the Lord. The intent of this letter is to encourage them to stay true to God even though they are suffering. God's grace is what is needed to stay in the fight to the end.

IT'S YOUR TURN

Below you will find two identical charts. One is for you to evaluate yourself in the areas that Peter addresses in this section of Scripture. The other is to be given to a friend, youth pastor, parent or someone else you trust. Ask the person to respond to how he or she sees you are growing and changing in these areas.

Honesty will be needed! After the chart is filled out, compare the two and see what differences there are. Ask the Lord to give you grace and guts to be willing to change and grow where there are weak points.

DIRECTIONS FOR YOU:

After each phrase, write down what level you think you are on: Playpen, K-5, Teenager, Adult or Coach/Trainer.

Lives in harmony _____

Sympathetic _____

Loves others _____

Compassionate _____

Humble _____

No repaying evil _____

Blesses others _____

Keeps tongue from evil _____

No deceitful speech _____

Does good, not evil _____

Seeks peace _____

Handles fear well _____

Heart set apart for Christ _____

Can present the gospel _____

Clear conscience _____

Model behavior _____

DIRECTIONS FOR OBSERVER:

After each phrase, write down what level you think the person you are evaluating is on: Playpen, K-5, Teenager, Adult or Coach/Trainer.

Lives in harmony _____

Sympathetic _____

Loves others _____

Compassionate _____

Humble _____

No repaying evil _____

Blesses others _____

Keeps tongue from evil _____

No deceitful speech _____

Does good, not evil _____

Seeks peace _____

Handles fear well _____

Heart set apart for Christ _____

Can present the gospel _____

Clear conscience _____

Model behavior _____

TAKING TIME BY THE THROAT

DC Talk sings a song on their *Free At Last* tape called "Time Is . . ." The gist in the message is that it is foolish to waste time, because the only time we can be assured of is the present. In a nutshell what Peter is saying in this paragraph is that we must spend our time on things that will last longer than we will. He addresses this in several ways:

- fight sin
- don't be overcome by evil
- live for God
- have godly values
- be aware of the judgment
- pray hard
- love others
- be aware of the end times
- be gracious
- don't grumble
- use the gifts God gave you

- serve others
- speak God's word

IT'S YOUR TURN

Instead of answering questions for this study, try this:

1. Record how you spend your time during the next two days. Include things like being in school, eating, sleeping, watching TV, listening to music, talking on the phone, etc.

2. At the end of the two days, add up how much time you spent on each activity.

3. Next, plan out how you will spend your time during the *next* two days. Select three things from the list included in this section and put them into your schedule.

4. At the end of this four-day experiment, see if there is a difference in how you spent your time.

TOUGH ASSIGNMENTS FROM GOD'S SCHOOL

Tough times often produce comments like: "This really stinks!" or "What did I do to deserve this?" or "I can't believe this is happening to me!" As we know, Peter is writing to people going through hard times. They have had their homes taken away and their possessions stolen. They are wondering how to handle the pain going on in their lives. Peter's instruction to them is interesting. He tells them to realize they are going through a test, a time of refinement. The application is easy to see. Just as there are pop quizzes and tests in school to show our progress, so there are tests in our walk with God to reveal what we are made of spiritually. These tests are not designed to hurt us and deflate us, but to show where we need to improve. When we view hard times that way, then we can graciously serve God and receive the guts to complete the tough assignments given us in God's school.

IT'S YOUR TURN

1. When was the last time you suffered unexpectedly because of your commitment to Christ? What happened?

2. Read 4:12 again. Do you think suffering is something you should expect?

3. Look up the following passages of Scripture and write down how they tie in with the gist of this lesson.

   James 1:2-4

   John 16:21

   2 Corinthians 12:7-10

4. Peter tells us to rejoice when we suffer for Christ's sake and that we are blessed when we are insulted for the name of Jesus. Who else in the Bible said that? (See Matthew 5:11 and Luke 6:22)

5. Have you ever met or read about someone who suffered for the cause of Christ? What happened to them? Did they have the grace and guts to endure?

6. The Bible speaks clearly about the judgment of God both for the believer (4:17) and for the whole world. Why do you think that will happen? See the following references: Psalm 58:11; Acts 17:31; Romans 2:16, 14:10; 2 Timothy 4:1; Hebrews 9:27; Jude 6.

7. Peter tells his followers that they should "commit themselves to their faithful Creator and continue to do good." What else should suffering people do? Would it make sense not to commit themselves to God?

8. How can suffering people be absolutely sure God will be there for them?

1 PETER 5:1-4

HOW TO BE A LEADER FOR THE LORD

H ave you ever met a leader and wondered how that person ever landed the job? At times leaders lead by intimidation, manipulation or guilt trips. That style of leadership is nothing more than an adult version of "King of the Hill." In fact, it isn't leadership at all, but dictatorship, and Adolf Hitler would have loved it.

Being a leader for the Lord is different. When a person is called to lead God's people, it means he or she is appointed by Him.

Several qualifications for spiritual leadership are revealed by Peter in this passage. Though he is addressing those who are in ministry and caring for the people in their churches, the passage is not limited to pastors. These characteristics should describe those who lead God's people in any capacity. Their lives should be marked by an ability to work alongside others, serve them and encourage them in the faith.

IT'S YOUR TURN

1. Have you ever met a leader who was a manipulator? Did this person have a strong following because of an ability to lay guilt trips on others?

2. Describe how a leader of God's people should be different from a manipulator.

3. As a leader in the New Testament church and a member of the disciples selected by Jesus, Peter could have "pulled rank" with those to whom he was writing. Why do you suppose he didn't do that?

4. Why should leaders of the Lord's people be willing, eager and meek?

5. Why shouldn't they be lazy or greedy? What if they are?

6. Review John 10:1-18, where Jesus talks about

the qualities of a good shepherd. List the verse(s) where He talks about:

a. honesty

b. concern for the sheep

c. trustworthiness

d. knowing the truth

e. giving his life for the sheep

f. commitment to the sheep

g. being the gate and the door

h. what robbers do

7. Suppose a leader has some of the qualities listed in John 10, but other qualities are missing. What should be done?

8. Peter says that when the Chief Shepherd (Jesus) appears, a crown of glory will be given that will never fade. What is he talking about? What do you think that day will be like?

9. Has the Lord placed you in some type of leadership at school, youth group, another organization or at work? If so, are you following the principles prescribed in 5:1-4?

STUDY 33

1 PETER 5:8-13

STANDING EYEBALL TO EYEBALL WITH THE DEVIL

The wise player always understands the way his or her opponent is going to play. When a competitor can be accurately predicted, the game is already won, though it may still be in session.

What is true in the world of sports is also true in the spiritual world. The only difference is that when you stand eyeball to eyeball with the devil, it is not a game—it's the real thing! Thankfully, God's grace supplies us with the guts to stand against Satan and defeat him. This formula isn't found in *USA Today* or *Seventeen*—or even the latest copy of *Sports Illustrated*. Only God's word tells us how to win over the devil.

IT'S YOUR TURN

1. How do you think the devil would like older people to be treated?

   __with respect   __humbly
   __with dignity   __as if they are stupid
   __with no regard or value
   __as if they are not "with it"

2. According to this passage, what will God do if people humble themselves under God's mighty hand?

3. Why is being humble under God's hand a necessary thing to do when we go to fight against the devil?

4. Why is the devil described here as a roaring lion? Why is he able to be resisted?

5. How do you suppose God will make us strong, firm and steadfast as we fight Satan by living holy lives?

6. Peter mentions three "veterans of war": Silas, Mark and himself. What major battles did these warriors face against the devil?

   a. Silas (Acts 16:16-40)

   b. Mark (Acts 15:36-41)

   c. Peter (John 18:15-18; 25-27)

7. It is important to understand the tactics of the devil. The Bible gives us a game plan on how to defeat him by revealing his characteristics and personal battle plan. The following passages tell the truth about the devil. Review them often and rejoice that you are on God's winning team!

THE TRUTH ABOUT OUR LYING ENEMY

His Fall	Ezekiel 28:11-19
His Sin	Isaiah 14:12-17
His Hierarchy	Ephesians 6:10-18
His Schemes	Genesis 3:1-7
His Deception	1 Timothy 4:1-8
His Perversion	Isaiah 5:18-23
His Imitation	2 Corinthians 11:1-15
His Activity in the Last Days	2 Thessalonians 2:1-12
His Desire to Hurt Us	Job 1:6-2:7
His Doctrine	2 Peter 1:16-2:22
His Response to the Word of God	Matthew 13:1-22
His Tempting Power	Luke 4:1-13, James 1:13-15
His Operation	Matthew 17:14-21

WHAT WE CAN COUNT ON

He is Defeated by Christ	Colossians 2:9-15
He is Destined to Hell	Revelation 20:1-10

9. While doing war with the devil is never easy, the great news is God promises us the grace and guts to stay in the fight. It will prove to be worth it. Notice how Peter concludes his letter: "Peace to all of you who are in Christ" (5:14).

2 PETER

INTRODUCTION

William Shakesphere nailed it when he said the lips of a dying man seldom lie. Second Peter is the last letter Peter wrote before he was put to death for his faith in Christ. The words flow from a man who knows his final days are near. In this short New Testament book, you will notice there is nothing soft and cozy laced throughout these words. With only 61 verses in the entire epistle, Peter cuts through any nonsense and "delivers the goods" concerning fake Christianity (chapter 1), false teachers (chapter 2) and what the future holds for the world (chapter 3). A simple way to understand Peter's last words would be by using the word "hope" as an acrostic:

Hang onto the truth you have been taught (1:12-13, 3:1-2).

Obey what you have seen and been made aware of (2:1-3; 3:17).

Passionately serve God (3:11-14).

Expect the return of Christ as the prophets foretold (3:12).

When we hope, we have reason to keep going. As believers, we have that assurance because we have Jesus, our ultimate hope.

IT'S YOUR TURN

1. Take 10 minutes and read Second Peter in one
   sitting. (You may even want to take more
   time and use two versions to get different
   perspectives.)

2. How would you evaluate Peter's writing?

   __kind words   __thoughtful
   __passionate   __sincere
   __"Hope I'm not too harsh, but . . ."
   __soft-spoken

3. Are there any similarities between First Peter
   and Second Peter? How would you describe
   the differences?

4. Suppose you were doing a newspaper article
   summarizing Second Peter. How would you
   break it down? (Be sure to include who,
   what, where, when, why and how)

PEACE, POWER AND PROMISES— THE THREE TENETS OF HOPE

When Peter wrote this second letter to the same churches who received his first letter, he was looking down the barrel of death. He knew his time to die was near; Nero was about to have him killed. Despite this rather grim reality, his words still express hope. He talks about grace and peace in 1:2 and says that "divine power has given us everything we need for life" (1:3). Furthermore, he speaks about the divine nature that those of us who believe can participate in. Where does all this come from? No other place but his hope in Christ. Result? He was still growing in the hope given to him by Christ, and he encouraged others in seven specific ways:

a. goodness to faith
b. knowledge to goodness
c. self-control to knowledge
d. perseverance to self-control
e. godliness to perseverance
f. brotherly kindness to godliness
g. love to brotherly kindness

IT'S YOUR TURN

1. Suppose you just found out that you have only five months to live. What would your emotions be?

2. Where do you believe Peter got his peace from? Do you think you would be as confident if you were in his sandals?

3. Did Peter somehow *earn* the peace and power he had to face death?

4. If you were in jail because of your faith in Christ, what promises would you lean on? What else would you do?

5. This passage talks about seven qualities in our spiritual life. Which of these are hard for you to practice?

__goodness   __knowledge   __love
__self-control   __perseverance
__godliness   __brotherly kindness

6. If these are practiced in our spiritual walk, what two things will we be kept from?

a.

b.

7. What three negative characteristics will invade a person who ignores this passage?

a.

b.

c.

8. What does Peter mean when he speaks of making our calling and election sure? How can we do that?

9. How can we be sure we will receive anything at the end of this life?

10. What do you think it means to receive a rich welcome into the eternal kingdom of Jesus?

ARE YOU SURE THAT YOU ARE SURE?

Few things are more frustrating than to discover what you thought was genuine was really a fake. Imagine finding out the jeans you paid $50 for were really rejects from a discount store! What if you discovered your $350 CD stereo was really only repackaged garbage from a toy store dumpster? People who spend their lives looking to crystals, tarot cards, mediums and psychics for help are in this situation. They really believe they are getting the real stuff, but according to Peter, only the Word of God is genuine. All else will end up in the dumpster of life.

IT'S YOUR TURN

1. Of what is Peter wanting to remind his friends in Second Peter 1:12?

2. Why do you suppose Peter is writing so in-

tensely about fakes?

3. How does having confidence in the Word of God give *us* confidence?

4. What proof does Peter offer that he is not following after "cleverly invented stories" about Christ?

5. What does Peter say he saw and heard on the mountain concerning Christ? How convinced was he that this was genuine and not a fake show?

6. Why shouldn't we place our faith in psychics, mediums or tarot cards?

7. What three forms of light is the Word of God

compared to in verse 19? What is everything else called?

a.

b.

c.

8. Where does Peter say Scripture comes from?

9. If Scripture came from God, how did the prophets receive it? What role did the Holy Spirit play?

10. Notice what else the Bible says about itself:

Psalm 19:7-8

Psalm 119:105

Isaiah 40:8

Matthew 4:4

Matthew 5:18

Romans 15:4

2 Timothy 3:15-16

Psalm 119:9-11

Hebrews 4:12

HOW TO SMELL A FAKE A MILE AWAY

Have you ever seen a boxer get KO'd—totally unconscious? Often the trainers or medical people will wave ammonia under the nose of the person and immediately the scent awakens him. In this chapter, Peter shifts gears from giving assurance about the teaching of Scripture to giving warnings about those who teach heresy. It is as though Peter has stepped into the ring and is waving smelling salts under the nose of his disciples, warning them to keep their guard up so they don't get KO'd by a false teacher.

IT'S YOUR TURN

1. Peter warns that false prophets are among the people. Since that is true, what do you think they would be teaching that is wrong?

2. According to 2:2, how will the false teachers present their heresies?

3. What is the difference between *teaching about* false prophets and *being* a false prophet?

4. What is it that Peter says fakes will bring on themselves? At what speed will that be delivered?

5. What happens to truth when false prophets follow false teachers?

6. Define "greed" and "exploit."

    a.

    b.

7. According to your definitions, how productive would it be for a true disciple to follow fake teachers who practice greed and exploit people?

8. Chapter one discusses the accuracy of the Bible. Chapter two discusses false teachers. What do you think is the connection between the two chapters?

9. What do "condemnation" and "destruction" mean here?

   a.

   b.

10. According to Second Peter 2:3, how do these words apply to fake teachers? Do you think God is just kidding?

TWO PICTURES OF THE SAME GOD

In the Gospels, there are "snapshots" of Jesus where He is portrayed as the gentle, compassionate, loving God that He indeed is. But He is also portrayed as the one who overturned the tables of the money changers and single-handedly drove them from the temple with His homemade whip. He also said the spiritual swindlers of His day, better known as the Pharisees, were nothing more than "whitewashed tombs, which look beautiful on the outside but on the inside are full of dead men's bones and everything unclean" (Matthew 23:27).

Just as there are two pictures of Jesus in the photo album of the Gospels, so there are two pictures of God in this passage of Second Peter. One is a picture of a God who is tender toward those who follow His truth. The other picture shows a God who is intolerant toward those who twist truth into false teaching.

IT'S YOUR TURN

1. In this passage, how is the Lord pictured as compassionate, and to whom is His compassion given?

2:5b

2:5c

2:7

2:9

2. How is the Lord portrayed as a judge, and who receives His judgment?

2:4

2:5

2:6

2:10-12

3. According to Peter's teaching, what was the result of God's compassion being shown toward people?

4. What was, or will be, the result of God exercising judgment?

5. Do you see the two pictures of God as conflicting? Why or why not?

6. Did God judge or condemn without first warning and pleading with people to repent? (Check one)

	YES	NO
a. ancient world	___	___
b. Sodom & Gomorrah	___	___
c. unrighteous	___	___

7. Is that compassionate?

8. How has God rescued you from trials?

9. What will be the punishment of false prophets and fallen angels?

10. Since God is against evil and will ultimately judge and remove it, how should we be living?

A FINAL WORD ABOUT FAKES— THEY DON'T FAKE OUT GOD

In a boxing match, a competitor always has an advantage if he can make his opponent think he is going to move one way when he is actually going to swing a different way. Mastering this fake-out often sends the contender to the mat, wondering how he got there.

In this passage, Peter delivers a knockout punch right up the middle. He doesn't dance around the ring and leave those watching him bored with the lull in the action. Instead, he lands a direct hit that earns every fake a 10-count. It is as though Peter has these words written on his gloves: Fakes Don't Fake Out God!

IT'S YOUR TURN

1. According to 2:13, what will happen to the fakes who harm the truth of the gospel? Who will deliver this knockout punch?

2. According to what Peter is saying, describe the eyes of fakes.

3. Review the story of Balaam in Numbers 22:4-20. Why do you think God would be willing to use a donkey to speak truth? What does that tell us about God's desire to have truth revealed to people?

4. In 2:17, Peter describes fakes as "springs with-

out water and mists driven by a storm." What would it be like to drink dust instead of water?

5. Imagine what it would be like to live in a cloudy mist. How clear would your vision be? How far away could you see?

6. Peter uses opposite terms to describe fakes. Think about his adjectives:

   2:18 they mouth empty, boastful words ("Words that sound impressive to the new convert but in reality have nothing to offer"—footnote from *NIV Study Bible*, Zondervan, 1985.)

   2:19 they promise freedom while they themselves are slaves

   2:20a they escaped corruption but are again entangled in it

   2:20b they are worse off at the end than they were at the beginning

7. The proverbs in verse 22 are pretty gross. What does Peter mean when he compares a dog licking up vomit to a fake Christian?

8. Why does a sow always wallow in mud? Why do fakes return to the filth of the world?

9. Think of any areas in your Christian walk that you might be faking. Spend some time in prayer asking God to help you change.

THE DAY SCOFFERS WILL WANT TO SKIP GOD'S SCHOOL

E ver since mandatory school attendance was put into law, playing hooky has been a favorite pastime of blockheads who don't want to learn. They would rather goof off than get with it educationally. Having a teachable spirit is simply beyond them.

In Second Peter 1, we saw how fake Christianity is not of the Lord. In chapter two Peter addresses fake prophets and teachers. In chapter three he discusses the future of the world. In the first seven verses he talks about the specific future of those who have laughed at Christianity and its teaching of the second coming of Jesus. From what Peter says, that will be a day when the scoffers will wish they could skip God's school. However, that won't be possible, and they will learn a lesson that day which their unteachable spirits will never forget!

IT'S YOUR TURN

1. In verse 1, Peter states he is writing this second letter to stimulate wholesome thinking. Why is that so important to us today?

2. According to 3:2, who are the three people Peter wants his readers to recall? What was so powerful about their words?

3. In keeping with our theme for this study, notice how 3:3-4 sounds like something from a current events class. Have you ever been mocked or heard about someone being mocked for his or her faith? What happened?

4. Peter also gives a history lesson in 3:5-6 by recounting the flood of Noah's time. In what ways did the flood change the world? Peo-

ple? History? How will the next judgment of God change things?

5. A concluding lesson is found in 3:7, where Peter gives a crash course in future projections. How can someone prepare for this "final exam" of judgment? Have you made your plans?

6. So far we have discussed how the scoffer will be taught a hard lesson on the day Jesus returns. Notice what Proverbs says about those who refuse to respond to God's word and why they won't repent.

   Proverbs 9:7   13:1

   14:6   15:12

   21:24   24:9

   3:34   9:8

7. Do you have a teachable spirit? Ask a teacher, your youth pastor and a parent to respond to this question.

8. There is a great deal of talk about the return
   of Christ. How would you advise someone
   to be ready for that? Are you ready?

STUDY 41

2 PETER 3:8-13

LEARNING TO TELL TIME— GOD'S WAY

What is the most exciting thing you have ever done? Been in a wedding? Had a date with the person of your dreams? Met a movie star? Been on TV? Shook hands with the President? Set a school record? Made straight A's?

Whatever has been the highlight of your life was probably something you looked forward to. The anticipation must have been hard to contain, and the clock must have seemed to go at turtle speed. But when the big moment came, everything else faded like cheap paint in desert sun. Suddenly the waiting was worth it all!

In this lesson, Peter addresses the day all Christians have been waiting for since Jesus first spoke of His return for the Church. While time seems to drag, we are reminded that the day of the Lord will be worth the wait. For those who were true to Christ, there will be no regrets!

IT'S YOUR TURN

1. Have you ever felt God was late? Delayed? Early? Why?

2. According to 3:8, how much time is one day to the Lord compared to our timetable?

3. What else could that mean?

4. Since 3:9 says God isn't slow, check off why you would say He hasn't returned yet.

__patient   __tardy   __indifferent
__likes making people angry
__wants people to repent   __merciful

5. Why does 3:10 refer to the coming of Christ as a thief?

6. What movie/video have you seen that gives you a mental picture of 3:10 when it says "the elements will be destroyed by fire"? Why?

7. Answer the question Peter asks in 3:11.

8. How does someone live a holy, godly life?

9. Are you looking forward to "the day of God"? Why or why not?

10. Do you want to live on a new earth? What will be the most exciting part for you? Is there someone you want to see there first? Are you taking anyone with you?

FOUR FINAL WORDS FROM A DYING MAN

When people know death is near they often make final preparations. Their words are chosen more carefully. Their will is put in order. Close friends and family members are contacted. As we already mentioned, William Shakespeare rang the bell when he said, "The lips of a dying man seldom lie."

In this final passage, Peter, who knew he was about to die, gives four final words to his friends. These are the most important things on Peter's mind, and he gave them not only to the early believers, but to us, too. Here they are:

a. Be found spotless, blameless and at peace with Him (3:14).

b. Remember that the Lord's patience equals salvation (3:15).

c. Be on your guard (3:17).

d. Grow in grace (3:18).

IT'S YOUR TURN

1. Why do you think Peter speaks so strongly at the end of his life?

2. How can someone be spotless? Blameless? At peace?

3. Why would Peter say the Lord's patience means salvation? Does that match up with anything Paul wrote about? (See Romans 2:4)

4. Peter says ignorant and unteachable people will distort passages of Scripture. Why do you think that would be a pattern of the unteachable?

5. What is the best way for a person to be on guard so he or she won't fall?

6. Peter speaks about a secure position. Who is the person he is writing about? What position does he speak about?

7. How secure is the position that a believer has?

8. What does it mean to "grow in grace"? How does that happen?

9. Why would Peter conclude his letter by saying "to him be glory both now and forever"?

10. Are you taking these final four words from Peter seriously?

WRAPUP

At the beginning of this study, we said living today is not easy. Without the grace and guts God gives us to live for Him, we would all be goners.

Perhaps you have wondered if God can bring *you* through the way He did the people in Hebrews and First and Second Peter. The best news you can hear today is not only *can* He do it, but He *will* do it! As we walk with Him in this life, looking to Him for all things, He will give us the grace and guts to serve Him. Stay true to Christ. No regrets! Just grace and guts to keep going. Go for it!